THE HOUSE THAT JACK BUILT

YURTS, TIPIS
AND BENDERS

THE HOUSE THAT JACK BUILT

YURTS, TIPIS

AND BENDERS

DAVID PEARSON

GAIA BOOKS LIMITED

A GAIA ORIGINAL

Books from Gaia celebrate the vision of Gaia, the self-sustaining living Earth,
and seek to help its readers live in greater personal and planetary harmony.

Original concept for 'The House that Jack Built' series: Joss Pearson
Project Editor and Research: Helena Petre
Copy Editor: Katherine Pate
Series Designer: Sara Mathews
Designer: Bridget Morley
Production: Lyn Kirby
Direction: Patrick Nugent

® This is a Registered Trade Mark of Gaia Books Limited

First published in the United Kingdom in 2001 by Gaia Books Ltd,
    66 Charlotte Street, London W1T 4QE
and 20 High Street, Stroud, Gloucestershire GL5 1AZ
Visit our website: www.gaiabooks.co.uk with on-line book shop

ISBN 1 85675 142 2

A catalogue record of this book is available from the British Library.

Printed and bound by Oriental Press, Dubai.

10 9 8 7 6 5 4 3 2 1

Cover image and page 2: by Hal Wynne-Jones: page 5: David Pearson

"To the nomad soul in all of us."

CONTENTS

CIRCULAR HOMES

"A MAN'S TENT IS LIKE A GOD'S TEMPLE."

(Kyrgyz proverb)

Today, many of us share a desire to be free and experience the pleasures of living lightly on the Earth. Like our nomadic ancestors, many of us have a deep inner yearning to roam with the seasons and be close to nature and the cosmos. The traditional forms of the yurt, tipi, and bender are the apogee of this experience and are far more satisfying than any modern Western-style tent. Being mainly circular in shape, they bring another dimension to the experience of free living – living in the round. It is difficult to define why circular spaces hold such a special magic and fascination. Maybe it is their natural affinity with the cycle of life – the movement of the sun, moon, and stars, and the cycle of the seasons. Maybe it is some archetypal memory of, and resonance with, former circle homes and round houses of our forebears. Whatever it is, you will be pleasantly surprised at the happy and peaceful effect that circular structures will have on you!

Nomadic populations usually live in some of the most inhospitable and barren regions of the world and this is why they are nomads. Whether it be the deserts of the Sahara and Gobi, the Central Asian steppe, or the polar tundras, these vast areas are either too hot and arid or too cold and windswept to be cultivated and support much population. Human inhabitants have little choice but to live off the scarce resources. These are quickly exhausted, so it is soon time to move or follow animal migratory routes. Peoples living in these conditions have to be remarkably ingenious and adaptable. This is shown in everything they do including the structures they build. An African grass-covered hut, a Romany gypsy "bender", an Asian yurt, or a Native American tipi, are all perfect lessons in appropriate design and sustainable building. Refined over generations, they are simple yet sophisticated, beautiful and comfortable.

YURT When British yurt-maker Hal Wynne-Jones spent his first night in a black felt yurt on the Anatolian plains he knew that he had "fallen in love for life". And it is this love for the yurt that has inspired Hal (page 28) and other innovative spirits such as Bill Coperthwaite in the USA (page 18), Stephanie Bunn in the UK (page 20), and Martien Van Zuilen in Australia (page 36) to make it their mission to bring the yurt and its crafts into Western life. Used today for everything from vacation accommodation to permanent homes, they also serve well as classrooms, meditation spaces, and saunas. Multi-celled yurts can be hired for exhibitions, wedding receptions, and conferences.

MONGOL NOMAD VILLAGE SHOWING MARRIAGE CEREMONY, HORSE CULTURE, CATTLE, CAMEL TRAIN, AND YURTS, PAINTED BY MONGOLIAN ARTIST P TSERENDORZH

The birthplace and real domain of the yurt, however, is the Central Asian Steppe. Over this vast area, stretching from the Caspian Sea, through Mongolia, and north into Siberia, the yurt is still the preferred home. The "yurt", meaning "dwelling", is home today to the majority of the Mongolian population. The capital Ulaan Baatar is actually surrounded by extensive yurt, or more correctly, *ger* suburbs. This is a region of little rain, strong winds, and very cold winters, where the temperature drops as low as −50°C. Traditionally, local peoples live a nomadic lifestyle based around the horse, camel, yak, and flocks of goats and *karakul* (fat-tailed) sheep. The sparse grazing requires herds to be moved to fresh pasture regularly. In the grazing season families housed in yurts spread out with their flocks over a large area, but in winter they gather together in a yurt camp in a sheltered spot to await spring.

The yurt is an ingenious portable circular structure covered with felt and canvas (see page 78) whose design has hardly changed since the time of Genghis Khan 800 years ago. More than just a house, the yurt has deep spiritual significance. It represents the universe in microcosm: the floor (the Earth), the roof (the sky), and the hole in the roof (the sun). It is oriented to the four corners of the Earth. The yurt also contains the five basic Asian elements: Earth (the floor) surrounded by Wood (the yurt frame), enclosing Fire (the hearth), surmounted by Metal (the grate), and Water (in the pot on the grate). The hearth, known as "the square of Earth", is sacred too, with its smoke rising up to the heavens.

A yurt has many advantages. It is strong, economical, and long-lasting. It is portable, self-supporting, and can even be moved fully erected. It can be fairly easily put up and taken down in about an hour. It does no permanent damage to the ground where it is pitched. The low roof height makes it inconspicuous. Its circular shape is aerodynamic and deflects the wind. It is easy to heat and keep cool. It can be made from local, environmentally friendly materials and, above all, it is secure, warm, and very comfortable.

TIPI   Inspired by such classic books as *The Indian Tipi* by Reginald and Gladys Laubin, a new generation of tipi lovers has spread the

MARY EVANS PICTURE LIBRARY

A DAKOTA ENCAMPMENT: S EASTMAN IN SCHOOLCRAFTS' *INDIAN TRIBES* **VOL 11**

word and experience of tipi living. This was the case with Dan and Emma Kigar who became "consummate tipi dwellers" and then went on to set up their own Colorado-based company (page 50). In England, Elizabeth Tom accepted a Sioux-style tipi in payment of a debt and then started a family vacation resort in a beautiful Cornish valley (page 58). Due to the efforts of such people, tipis are now more popular than ever.

Unlike the yurt, the North American tipi is no longer used by its originators – the Native Americans of the Great Plains. This huge area of rolling grassland, which extends from Texas to southern Canada and eastward from the Rocky Mountains to the Mississippi River, was once inhabited by vast herds of buffalo and other animals. Before the onslaught of colonial settlers from the east, this was the home and hunting grounds of many tribes of nomadic and semi-nomadic peoples. At that time, before the introduction of the horse via Mexico, large dogs were used to transport tipis. But the advent of the horse radically changed all this and, with its increased mobility, made a permanent nomadic lifestyle (and larger tipis) possible.

After over-wintering in small groups in sheltered woods and valleys, the whole tribe would gather in great spring camps to celebrate rituals such as the Sun Dance and prepare for the buffalo hunts. These camps often numbered one to two thousand tipis, arranged in four or five concentric circles. They measured up to a mile (1.5 km) in diameter and, like a tipi, had their entrance facing east. Buffalo supplied almost every need from food and clothes to tools (horn and bone), and fuel (dung), as well as the covering and bindings for the tipi. With the onset of winter, the tipi camps were struck, everything packed in small bundles and moved by horse and *travois* – two

MARY EVANS PICTURE LIBRARY

CAMP OF THE CHIPPEWA PEOPLE FROM *LETTERS AND NOTES ON THE MANNERS, CUSTOMS AND CONDITIONS OF THE NORTH AMERICAN INDIANS* BY GEORGE CATLIN

poles with a platform between them, dragged behind a horse or dog.

A tipi is one of the most sophisticated portable homes ever devised (page 84). The interior layout has certain similarities with that of the yurt: the floor represents the Earth, the curving tipi walls evoke the sky, and the poles link Earth to the spirit world of Wrakan'Tanka, the Great Mystery. For comfort, a lining called a "dew cloth" is hung around the inside of the frame to reduce draughts, provide insulation, and increase smoke ventilation.

BENDER In Europe, and especially the UK, the bender has undergone a recent renaissance. This modest domed structure – the simplest circle home – is used both as temporary and as semi-permanent homes by people leading alternative lifestyles – travelling folk, the homeless, and protesters such as at Fairmile, England (page 70). Often hidden from view in woods, disused quarries, and waste ground, they are usually built from free scrap and recycled materials. If not evicted, the occupants will live year-round in these structures as do members of the Kings Hill Collective, England (page 66),

where official permission has been granted for these "low-impact" homes to remain.

Benders are not new. Such simple domed shelters built of bent-over saplings covered with grass, woven mats, bark, or cloth (page 90) have been in use all across the world since prehistoric times. More recently, in Europe, they were shelters for Romany gypsies, and in North American woodlands the wigwam was the Native American version. Covered with bark sheets or reed mats, these varied from a 12–15 ft (3.5–4.5 m) diameter Algonquin or Chippewa family house to the impressive 100 ft (30 m) communal longhouse of the Iroquois and Huron tribes of the St Lawrence River and Lake Ontario region. Another variation, the *wikiup*, served as a winter house of the Kikapoo tribe and a temporary summer camp for the Apache.

To get started on building your yurt, tipi, or bender, look at the Make It section (page 78) for basic guidance. For details of courses and workshops, and companies who supply kits, consult the Resources section (page 92). Whether you choose yurt, tipi, or bender, start today and find your path to your circle home.

AT HOME IN MONGOLIA

Paul King: The inspiration for my first yurt came from six photographs in *National Geographic,* showing two Mongolians assembling a wooden frame and fitting felt to produce a sturdy home, or *ger.* Over the next seven years I made yurts, learning from mistakes and improving each one. Still, there were many questions to which I could find no answers. How do the Mongolians produce that slightly conical wall profile? Why are roof poles round at the bottom but square at the top? To find out, I went to Mongolia.

As the plane began its slow descent, tiny white dots appeared, thinly scattered over the unbroken green of the steppe. These proved to be yurts, sited individually or in small groups, surrounded by sheep, cattle, and horses. The suburbs of Ulaan Baatar stretched out for miles, consisting almost entirely of *gers* in small fenced compounds. Clearly I had come to the right place.

A quick lesson in Mongolian taught me the names of all the components of a *ger*: each trellis wall section is a *khana*, the roof wheel is the *tono*, and each roof pole is a *uni*. At the Ulaan Baatar yurt factory I was shown the display yurt, a top-of-the-range 21 footer (6.4 m) beautifully painted with two sets of wooden doors.

When I met Khart Dorj, a *ger* maker from the Mongolian Artisans' Union, he was working on a 12 ft (3.7 m) *ger*. The larch frame was complete but undecorated. He showed me a finished *tono* and a door carved with Buddhist and Shamanic designs and painted with bright lacquers. Good carving can increase the cost of a yurt tenfold.

PAUL KING

L: A NEW FACTORY-MADE *GER* WITH TRADITIONAL DECORATION TR: THE RAISED *TONO* (CROWN) WAS FORMERLY USED TO DRAW OUT SMOKE BR: LIFE IN THE INTERIOR OF A GOBI NOMAD'S *GER*

Having seen new *gers* and factories, it was time to meet some real nomads in their yurts. My time in the Gobi Desert was spent visiting nomad *gers*. When visiting a *ger*, first make sure the dog is under control and then just walk in; to knock is to question the host's hospitality and is most impolite.

Most Gobi nomad families buy their yurt frame and make their own felt cover. It takes two weeks to make an entire cover, which should last twenty years. They move frequently, transporting the *ger* by camel, and expect the frame to last ten years. I saw one family moving house: they simply left the furnishings in place and once the *ger* was disassembled, everything was left outside, ready to pack.

In early October the nomads in the more fertile and forested North were preparing for winter. Families assemble their *gers* on timber platforms in sheltered valleys. The *gers* are insulated with up to six layers of felt and the metal stove is kept burning continually. Here, where *gers* are moved on ox-carts about five times a year, frames are expected to last a lifetime, but felt covers last about five years.

I left Mongolia as the snow started to fall. Once home, I wasted no time in putting my new-found knowledge to use. I built a new 18 ft (5.5 m) Mongolian-style *ger* using round-shafted roof poles with tapering tops. Having bent the wall poles to produce slightly sloping sides, I crowned it with a smooth, curved eight-spoked *tono*. The result is an authentic, aesthetically pleasing *ger*, in which my partner and I were married in the spring.

PAUL KING

T: DISMANTLING THE GOBI DESERT *GER* IN PREPARATION FOR MOVING B: DOWN COMES
THE *GER*, LEAVING THE CONTENTS READY FOR PACKING

BUILDING A WAY OF LIFE

Dan Neumeyer: I built my first yurt with Bill Coperthwaite almost thirty years ago. It was clear to me then, even as a 10-year-old, that Bill was not just designing buildings, but a way of life – close to nature, simple, nourishing – one that has inspired me ever since.

A *National Geographic* article in 1962 first impressed Bill with the folk genius in the design of the traditional yurt. He found in this structure both a rich potential for creative design and an opportunity for developing a simple dwelling that people could build themselves. Since then, Bill has used yurt building as a teaching tool with school groups and families around the world. A few of his students have started companies making yurts commercially, but Bill's interest has always been with the process of design. For him, helping people create something themselves is as important as the finished structure.

Though every yurt Bill constructs has unique features, some consistent elements have emerged. These include wooden walls, which are better suited than felt or canvas to climates with heavier precipitation. Another trademark is the outward sloping wall, which creates a more comfortable angle to sit against and makes the building seem smaller from the outside and more spacious inside. Bill also uses an insulated double wall for some larger yurts. His concentric design provides a means of dividing the space while retaining the integrity of the circle.

Almost forty years after building the first yurt in the West, Bill still makes design discoveries with every endeavor. I still join him as often as I can.

JADE YURTS

T: LIBRARY AND RESIDENCE, DICKINSON'S REACH, BUCKS HARBOR, MAINE (CONCENTRIC YURT)   BL: YURT AT UNIVERSITY OF NEW HAMPSHIRE (JEWEL YURT)   B: GUEST HOUSE, DICKINSON'S REACH, BUCKS HARBOR, MAINE (EMERALD YURT)

LIVING WITH YURT FRAME-MAKERS

Stephanie Bunn: As a novice anthropologist, I went to Kyrgyzstan to learn about yurts through living with people who make and live in them.

The Kyrgyz call their yurt a *boz uy*, or "grey home" because they are afraid that calling them *ak uy*, "white home" might cause the white felt covering to become grey, like a poor shepherd's tent. Masters known as *uychu* (*uy* maker) or *djygachy* (woodworker) make the frames.

I lived for one autumn with the Ismailovs, a family of *boz uy* makers. At this time, Sapar did most of the work, helped by his son Irydan. Sapar's father, Toktosun, had been a well known master across the region. He had taught twelve men in his village how to make *boz uy*, so the whole village was known as a "school" for yurt masters.

Learning to make a *boz uy* takes one month, as long as it takes to make the frame, but an apprentice will spend a year learning to manage the willow from which they are made; to steam the poles in fermenting sheep's dung; to bend the wood in a special hand-made device; to stain the frame; to bend the crown, and so on.

Ironically, *boz uy* makers are rarely nomadic herders themselves, but live a settled life in valley villages. However, I also lived in the high mountains with a family of shepherds headed by a remarkable man, Alpymysh *ata*. He had learned as a teenager to make tent frames by watching a local master, and then made his own. In this, he and his family had lived each summer for many years, when they went to the high mountain pastures with their animals.

STEPHANIE BUNN

TL: TOKTOSUN ISMAILOV, *BOZ UY* MASTER, AT WORK ON THE TRELLIS BL: ALPYMYSH OROZALIEV'S FAMILY ERECTING THEIR *BOZ UY* IN THE HIGH MOUNTAIN PASTURES R: ALPYMYSH *ATA* HOLDING UP THE CROWN

FELTMAKING IN KYRGYZSTAN

The tent covers are made from felt by the wife of the family who lives in them. In this way she shows what a good wife she is. The felt covers are costly both in terms of the fleeces from which they are made, and in terms of time. Felt is a fundamental nomad fabric in Central Asia, and has been found preserved in archeological remains from 2500 years ago. It is made from sheep's wool, using a simple technology that is easy to transport. It is warm, has strong insulating properties, and is wind- and waterproof.

I learned feltmaking with three Kyrgyz families, staying with them over two summers. As well as making the white tent covers, many women are skilled at making felt carpets. With vibrant colours and a "mosaic"-style design, these carpets are uniquely Kyrgyz. Most women have most of the skills involved, but the women who are especially talented at drawing the patterns are called *usta* or "masters". The women I worked with had learned from their mothers, making the beautiful carpets later given to them on their wedding days. From these they would never be parted.

To make a basic pressed felt, the fluffed-up fleece is laid out on a sedge mat, with the coloured pattern of dyed fleece arranged on top. Then the wool is sprinkled with boiling water and rolled up in the mat like a swiss roll. This roll is kicked up and down, usually by men and women, for about one hour. Then it is spread out and the felt is rolled using elbows for a further half hour. Finally, the helpers relax and enjoy refreshing drinks or a meal.

STEPHANIE BUNN

TL: DESIGN LAID OUT FOR A KYRGYZ PRESSED FELT TR: THE COMPLETED LAID OUT PATTERN BL: MEN KICKING THE FELT UP AND DOWN A MOUNTAIN BR: FINISHING OFF THE FELT USING ELBOW ROLLING

THE BEST GUEST YURTS

One of the most remarkable events during my visit to Kyrgyzstan was a festival dedicated to the Kyrgyz ancestral hero, Manas, who led the Kyrgyz back to their motherland in the Tien Shan mountains 1000 years ago. This festival in 1995 drew people from all the different Kyrgyz tribes from Kyrgyzstan, China, Tajikistan, and beyond. During the Soviet period such gatherings of nomadic peoples were actively discouraged, and this was the first event of its type since independence. Here all the best guest yurts from the different regions were erected.

Although the most usual name for the Kyrgyz yurt is *boz uy*, the word *uy* (home) can be adapted to describe all possible variations of felt tent. *Konok uy* means guest home, while *chong uy* means big tent. The tents at the Manas festival were mostly of these two types. Inside a *konok uy* the decorations are made to the highest possible quality. There are felt carpets and a vibrant display of bedding, coloured bands of patterned felt, embroidery, and weaving around the lower roof walls, embroidered silk hangings, as well as bags and textile shelves. Providing such comforts for guests confers prestige on the householders.

The most remarkable tent at the Manas festival was a three-storey yurt, built by a group of artisans for welcoming foreign dignitaries. In the past, some yurt masters built great festival tents, made of three or four tents attached to each other, with interconnecting doors. However, the skill and knowledge needed to make such tents is rarely found these days.

STEPHANIE BUNN

T: THREE-STOREY YURT AT THE MANAS FESTIVAL IN KYRGYZSTAN BL: DECORATIONS ON A *CHONG UY*, WITH TUFTS OF YAK HAIR BR: FELT TENT DECORATIONS AROUND A YURT AT THE MANAS FESTIVAL

"ONCE UPON A TIME..."

My interest in the Kyrgyz *boz uy* came about through working with children as an artist. I used to work for a horse-drawn theatre company touring rural Britain and Ireland. "How great it would be," I thought, "to create a felt storytelling yurt made by and for children." I visited some feltmakers in Hungary who advised me and, in 1988, with the help of the theatre company and ninety schoolchildren, I made my first yurt. The children made the felt, creating all the designs inspired by nomadic stories, while the adults steam-bent the wood and joined together the willow frame. As they worked the children sang and beat drums, and we had great celebrations and storytelling in the finished yurt.

Since then, I've made many other yurts with different organisations and groups of children – from city farms to museums and art galleries. Some are used for storytelling, some for classrooms, and some for exhibitions. The yurt is a marvellous space for children to hear stories about other cultures.

Nowadays when I take on such projects Hal Wynne-Jones (see page 28) makes the frames, and I make the felt and concentrate on showing children about Kyrgyzstan, and telling stories. Recently I developed a four-bay yurt made by Hal at the Earth Centre, Doncaster, England, into a space where children could learn about the yurt, nomadic life, and sustainability. In a similar project my friend and colleague, Christina Sargent, travelled to the remote Scottish Orkney Islands, working with 350 children to make the "Orkney yurt" for the islands' festival.

STEPHANIE BUNN

TL: BEES AND FARM ANIMALS CUT OUT FROM WOOL AND LAID INTO A PATTERN TR: CHILDREN LAYING OUT FELT PATTERNS BASED ON A CENTRAL ASIAN STORY BL: CHILD'S PATTERN BASED ON AN AFRICAN CREATION MYTH BR: FELT YURT MADE BY CHILDREN AT A CITY FARM

L O V E   Y U R T S

Hal Wynne-Jones: The first night I spent in a black felt yurt on the Anatalolian plains I knew that I had fallen in love for life. I knew then that I wanted to pursue the craft of yurt making as far as my own limits, so it had to become my livelihood as well as my passion. As a result, over the past 13 years I have ended up in situations I could never have dreamed of, not always pleasant, not always apparently fruitful, but never routine or boring.

As a builder and traveller (and born under the sign of Cancer!) the yurt was for me the most sublime archetype any dwelling could aspire to. Translocating this Central Asian housing staple into the long damp British winter/summer has led to many experiments in the design details and practical usage of the yurt. This problem solving is in itself very satisfying, if painfully laborious and ruinously expensive.

My initial hope was to provide low cost, low impact but comfortable and secure housing. This has been a qualified success. There are hundreds of people in the UK alone living in yurts full time, but very few of those have bought them off the peg from me. A far greater number have built their own after courses or at workshops. An even larger number have built their own independently as awareness and respect for these remarkable structures spreads. This leaves me supplying mainly the luxury market in second homes, which gives me the freedom to refine the craft processes and detailing to the point where eventually (I hope) the yurt can be integrated completely into the British vernacular.

HAL WYNNE-JONES

THE EARTH CENTRE AT DONCASTER, ENGLAND: THE MULTI–CELLED *GER* IS A FLEXIBLE STRUCTURE
THAT LENDS ITSELF TO ALL KINDS OF LARGE GATHERINGS AND SETTINGS

I started to develop the multi-celled yurt in 1990 and this now constitutes at least half of my business. I rent it out for a wide range of functions: story-telling festivals, weddings, memorial services, exhibitions, concerts, and even a Turkish bath and sauna complex. Ironically, the hire aspect of the business is the closest to the original nomadic spirit that drew me to yurts in the first place. I love arriving at dawn on a bare, wind- and rainswept field, everything packed tight in the Transit van camel. By nightfall the yurt is up, warm and weathertight, lights twinkling, music playing, rugs and cushions laid out ready to receive the first guests. By the following evening everything is packed away again and we are off to the next pasture. The field is back to bare earth and sky – was it a dream?

The Kyrgyz say you should move your yurt before you have worn away the grass at the threshold. Many yurt dwellers now live semi-permanently on one site, and the nomadic aspect has been lost. So it is important to me that I keep contact both with the amazingly versatile portability and the rigorous responsibility of constructing an absolutely secure family home.

My interest now lies in developing a system of four orbital sites around an ordinary town, for yurt dwellers moving to a four-seasonal rhythm. The aim is to combine the continuity necessary for earning a living, raising children, etc, with the self-cleansing lifestyle of the frequent mover. As the system is permanent, but the individual sites temporary, any local opposition should be assuaged.

HAL WYNNE-JONES

PATTERNS OF LIGHT AND SHADE, CROWN AND CANVAS, PLAY INSIDE THE MULTI–CELLED *GER*

GROW YOUR OWN HOME

Peter Whiteman: Few of us have entered a yurt and not fallen under its spell. The simple design, proven over two millennia of use, wonderfully combines function and beauty, representing the pinnacle of nomadic architecture. It is well adapted to both the climate and the available raw material resources of the Central Asian Steppes and mountains, and the need for a mobile home. Blending the virtues of a tent – quick to erect and stable – with those of a house – spacious and draught-free, light and airy – the circular structure fosters feelings of comfort and security.

How did I get involved? Having had the privilege to work as an agronomist in the Hindu Kush and Karakorum mountains, I have always since been fascinated by the lands of the snow leopard and of the pastoral peoples who share its environment in Central Asia, the yurt-dwelling Kyrgyz, Khazak, and Mongol people. So when ten years ago I actually saw a real yurt in England (displayed by Hal Wynne-Jones at the Whole Earth Show) my heart leapt and I resolved to acquire one. Hal has done much to popularise the yurt in the UK, simplifying its design and running courses in making the framework. After attending one of his courses, I returned home to my farm and gathered the necessary materials from within my borders.

We operate our farm organically and our guiding principle is to use our own resources sustainably. So for us the yurt became the ultimate low cost, environmentally-kind housing. We sourced the willow poles for the framework, the ash for the roof hoop,

PETER WHITEMAN

L: FELT LAID OUT FOR ROLLING, TO HARDEN IT TR: FLUE FROM WOODBURNER, SEEN AGAINST CROWN
BR: WALL-FELT CLADDING FOR LIGHT SUMMER USE

and the oak for the door posts from our hedgerows, and used our sheep's fleeces for the cladding. It gave us great satisfaction to grow our own house! The unwanted tops of the willow poles were planted out as cuttings to form a small plantation that will yield us a continuous supply of coppiced poles.

I wanted to create the yurt as ethnically authentically as possible, so I used only hand tools to cleave and shave the various components, and fastened them together with pegs, wedges, and rawhide thong. Rawhide is not available commercially, so I had to make it from the hide of a casualty calf that I had previously preserved by salting. It makes strong and tight yet flexible joints in the trellis wall section. Even now, every time I put up the yurt, I secretly hope someone is watching when I spectacularly expand the two-foot (60 cm) wide trellis to form an 18 ft (5.5 m) long arc in a couple of seconds. I used only naturally coloured fleece for the pattern, which depicts a Kyrgyz symbol of ram's horns, eagle's claws, and running dogs.

Besides its obvious use for family and group camping, I also use the yurt for a variety of other purposes – field office, workshop, medieval archery pageants, as a stall at shows selling vegetables, or demonstrating wood-craft (the unusual stall attracts more customers!), and as an invaluable instant spare room when those extra visitors arrive. I cannot rise to yaks and bactrian camels for transport, but it all fits snugly into the back of my pick-up, and makes a refreshing alternative to a conventional caravan when touring.

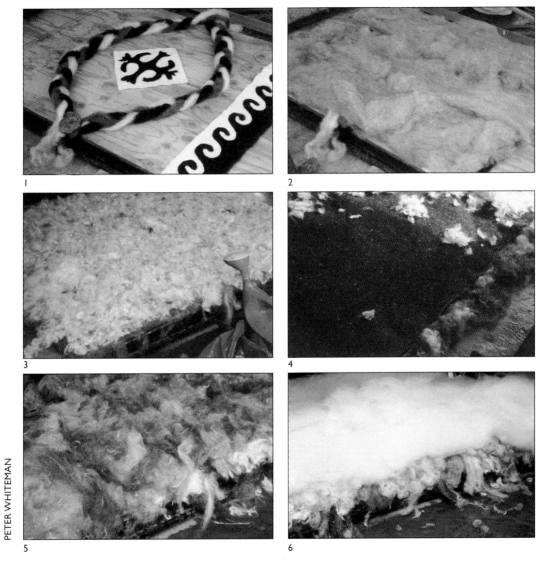

PETER WHITEMAN

STAGES OF FELTING: 1, 2 LAYING OUT PATTERN, STABILISING PATTERN 3, 4 LAYERS OF HAND-PLUCKED
WOOL AND GARDEN MULCH 5, 6 MORE WOOL AND A FINAL LAYER OF WHITE CARDED WOOL

THE ART OF THE YURT: AUSTRALIA MEETS MONGOLIA

Martien Van Zuilen: In 1998 I coordinated an Australian Community Art project to build a Mongolian style ger (yurt), supported and assisted by The Australian Forum for Textile Arts. I am a feltmaker, community artist, and tutor. As part of an overseas research tour I travelled to Mongolia in 1997, where I observed the traditional feltmaking process. I stayed in yurts and learned first-hand about their structure, purpose, and importance in the harsh Central Asian climate. I returned with a wealth of information and a desire to share my experiences with as many people as possible.

The yurt building project involved over 150 people right across Australia, and took almost four months to complete. During this time I covered over 7,500 miles (12,000 km) and travelled to five different states, where groups of feltmakers gathered to make large pieces of felt. We used feltmaking techniques that closely followed traditional processes, even using a horse to pull the felt rolls along "Mongolian-style". The fleeces were donated by sheep-breeders; it took 220 lbs (100 kg) of fleece to make the felt coverings.

During these yurt-building travels, I gave talks and workshops on my time in Mongolia. Through these the project also addressed the topic of "shelter", that is, the ways in which we live and what we need physically, emotionally, or materially, to survive. It soon became clear that "shelter" is much more than just a roof overhead.

Melbourne-based woodworker Kerry Bryan gave generously of her time to design and construct the major

MARTIEN VAN ZUILEN

WOODWORKER KERRY BRYAN HELPED DESIGN AND MAKE THE FRAME: LATTICE, PLANTATION OREGON; WHEEL, RECLAIMED ELM; DOOR FRAME, RECYCLED PINE, OREGON; ROOF POLES, SYCAMORE.

part of the framework, based on my slides and photographs from Mongolia, as well as drawings from books. The frame is made from plantation oregon (lattice walls), reclaimed elm (central wheel), recycled pine and oregon (door frame and support posts), and sycamore (roof poles). The lattice wall pieces are steam-bent and tied with leather ties in traditional Mongolian style. With a 16 ft (4.8 m) diameter, a central height of 9 ft (2.7 m), and walls 5 ft (1.5 m) high, it is a full-scale Mongolian yurt.

It took four months to build the yurt and for the dream to become reality. The sheer energy required to build it, the respect that participants showed for one another, and the fact that people were dependent on one another to finish the project, fully expressed the philosophy behind the project, more clearly than any words could. It touched the lives of many involved and those who witnessed its growth and completion.

The yurt now travels around Australia in true nomadic style, with me as caretaker. I have erected it at textile-related conferences and festivals and at many schools, where children of all ages have been able to learn at first-hand about life in another culture. Our yurt has been the focus of community-based arts and crafts festivals, and workshops on yurts and feltmaking. It continues to form a "meeting place within a meeting", inviting people to gather, share, and participate within it. In this way, it is very much a living, working exhibit and it continues to tell its story as it travels.

MARTIEN VAN ZUILEN

FELT COVERINGS WERE MADE WITH FLEECES DONATED BY SHEEP-BREEDERS ACROSS AUSTRALIA

KEEPING THE YURT IN THE FAMILY

Alex Walshaw: After spending cold Welsh winters in tipis, the warm, spacious conditions of a yurt are most inviting. I first experienced yurts while visiting a forester friend in Bangor, North Wales, and was inspired to build one of my own. I'd entered his yurt on a freezing cold day, to encounter a blazing woodburner and definite T-shirt temperatures.

Not long afterward I attended a yurt-making weekend course with Hal Wynne-Jones (see page 28). I ended up staying three months, building my own yurt with Hal's expert guidance. I used ash and willow for the crown, with a lattice of sweet chestnut wood. I then covered the frame in sturdy green canvas.

Returning to Wales, I set up the yurt on a friend's smallholding. Yurt life was warm, comfortable, and sociable when friends visited for musical evenings.

As long as I had a good pile of dry firewood, everything kept snug throughout the winter. I cooked on a small gas stove or outside over an open fire, and became adept at making stews and crumbles, and drinking many mugs of tea.

Lights-out time was unique as the moonlight poured in through the "skylight" and I slept soundly until the first sunrays awoke me, prompting me to throw twigs on the fire and brew tea. Of course it was not all fun and games, and squatting over a hole with damp toilet paper was arduous. Lack of hot water eventually drove me back to bricks, mortar, and electricity after a total of three satisfying years spent in a bender, tipi, and finally a yurt.

HAL WYNNE-JONES

THE YURT THAT ALEX BUILT, NOW INSTALLED ON HIS FATHER'S DAIRY FARM IN LINCOLNSHIRE, ENGLAND

Chris Walshaw: When my son Alex first mentioned his plans to sell the yurt and move to Cornwall, I was very concerned. I'd visited him frequently and associated the yurt with a special time in his young life. My disappointment that this wonderful handmade structure was to leave our family prompted me to buy it. The impulse overtook me not because I contemplated yurt dwelling, but because I wanted to retain the yurt for Alex's future use.

So the yurt was expertly stored at Hal's barn, I paid the storage fee, and continued my farming life. Several years later, a kind friend delivered the yurt to my Lincolnshire home. We erected it immediately, and that evening I moved a mattress in and slept there for the first of many wonderful late summer nights. Little did I know that I'd still be sleeping in my son's work of art as winter turned to spring. Entertaining evenings followed, spent with friends Mongolian overtone-chanting in the unique acoustics. Before long, the yurt became a significant part of my life.

I fitted a new logburning stove and chimney, and gathered fine rugs for the floor. I've experienced all weathers in the yurt and am thoroughly enjoying my circular space. My general health has improved, and colds are a thing of the past. Most of all, I appreciate the closeness to nature, the sounds of the night, and my own deep peaceful sleep as I breathe clear cold air. If I hear a cow in labour on the farm, I can swiftly assist. I am amazed how well yurt life blends with my farm work, and my spiritual side has been awakened.

CHRIS WALSHAW

CHRIS'S YURT MAKES AN UNUSUAL YEAR–ROUND BEDROOM, WHILE THE ACOUSTICS ARE IDEAL
FOR SPRING AND SUMMER MUSIC SESSIONS

HOLIDAY YURTS FOR HIRE

ta allan: From a humble beginning in the early 1990s – a few circular tents situated in a couple of parks – Oregon now offers, for a nominal rental charge, a total of 146 yurts in fifteen of the state's nineteen coastal parks and five inland state parks.

All of the yurts have wooden floors and decks. The windows are covered with thick plastic and screens. Flaps are roll-up, tie-down style. (Be sure to roll them "under" not "over" … you'll save yourself a shocking shower when you let them back down.)

The yurts used are manufactured by Pacific Yurts, of Cottage Grove, Oregon. Wooden lattice walls are covered by thick vinyl cloth. The yurts are kept cool in summer by a ceiling fan and cross winds, and warm in winter thanks to a small space heater.

Whether nestled under giant Douglas fir trees away from the coastal winds, perched on a cliff overlooking the vast Pacific Ocean, or plopped right down on the beach, sleeping in a yurt is a unique experience.

By day, the yurts provide a bright and cheery environment. At twilight, stars begin to twinkle through the center skylight. Once fully darkened, the night sky comes alive as sparkling stars begin a nocturnal dance. Constellations pass over and shooting stars fall right through your peripheral vision. With luck, come the morning, the dozens of native and migratory birds provide an aerial puppet show, backlit by dawn, across the same dome.

And all the while, the comforting tune of the ocean is heard, lapping the coast below.

TA.ALLAN

YURTS FOR HIRE AT OREGON'S STATE PARKS, USA; BLUE SKY AVAILABLE IN SEASON

PEACEFUL VALLEY YURTS

Jane Taka: In 1993 my brother Ian and I returned to Turkey, the country of our childhood. With my Turkish husband, Tanfer, we began creating a holiday retreat in southern Turkey called Huzur Vadisi (Peaceful Valley). We wanted to build accommodation that would reflect and preserve Turkic culture, which extends from Mongolia to modern Turkey. We also wanted our spaces to blend into the landscape and create a sense of intimacy with nature.

The yurt has survived more than a thousand years. Like all successful designs, this is due to its simplicity and functionality – the bentwood frames, domed roof, and portability cannot be refined further. Yurt design also has a spiritual dimension: the central hearth represents the Earth under the open roof wheel, the so-called "eye of heaven". Sleeping under this eye, seeing the stars and moon wheel overhead, is one of the greatest pleasures of the yurt. Enclosed in its circular womblike walls, you feel linked to all the nomadic peoples who have shared a similar space over the centuries.

To make our yurts we scoured Turkey for the right materials. For the frames we cut chestnut saplings from a coppiced forest on the shores of the Black Sea, 600 miles (1,000 km) away. They were transported from the forest by camel, and then by truck to the south. These poles were hand stripped, sanded, steamed in a home-made boiler, then bent to create the arched roof supports. They were then oiled, and to create our six original yurts, 10,000 holes were drilled for the cords to tie the latticework sides together.

JANE TAKA

PERFECTLY POSITIONED TO BLEND IN WITH THE ENVIRONMENT, HUZUR VADISI'S YURTS
ARE TUCKED AWAY AMONGST THE OLIVES AND PINES

Traditionally yurts are covered with the oldest of known fabrics, woollen felt. A wonderful insulating material, it keeps out heat and cold. We began our quest for a feltmaker who could make the vast quantities we needed. Felt is still used in Turkey for smaller items but hasn't been used in quantities like ours for at least a generation. Each of our yurts is 16 ft (5 m) in diameter and about 10 ft (3 m) in height, and we needed 430 square yards (360 sq m) of felt. In the town of Afyon we finally found the valiant Ahmet Vatandas, a traditional feltmaker, who promised to help us. Our felt was made in a little medieval workshop, where the only concession to modernity was the big steam pump which beat the wool fibres into a matted pulp. Ahmet designed a traditional pattern in the felt, made of contrasting black wool. This is now the Huzur Vadisi logo.

The postscript is that, after twice replacing the felt, we finally had to give in (as do many native yurt dwellers) and cover the yurts with canvas. This was because everything that walked, nibbled, and flew wanted to eat or steal the felt for nesting. The yurts now have a different but equally lovely atmosphere. The pattern of the olive leaves can be seen from inside the yurts dappling the canvas, and at night the yurts glow softly like enormous Chinese lanterns on their trellis framework. We also made two smaller yurts, influenced by a modern Kazhakstani yurt, using machine-cut poles, brightly painted, to create a different, more ethnic feel, in contrast to the natural colours and oiled wood frames of the larger yurts.

TANFER TAKA

TANFER TAKA

IAN WORRALL

TL: THE CROWN OF CHESTNUT SAPLINGS TR: MAKING FELT BY HAND STARTS WITH
FLUFFING UP THE WOOL TO MAKE IT EVEN B: CLOSE TO NATURE AT HUZUR VADISI

SUSTAINABLE SHELTERS, SURPRISING SOLUTIONS

Dan and Emma Kigar: Back in 1975, the "back to the land" movement was in full swing. We were living in Michigan, outside Ann Arbor, on a 4,500 acre (200 ha) unroaded wilderness parcel, and we decided to build our first tipi to provide affordable housing while Emma completed her BA in Environmental Studies. It was soon donated to the Earthworks alternative school, the namesake for our tipi line. Shortly afterward, we packed up and moved to Breckenridge, Colorado, and lived there year-round in a tipi for three years at an elevation of 11,300 ft (3,400 m). We became consummate tipi dwellers and fledgling entrepreneurs as we began making tipis for friends and neighbors.

As Breckenridge became more urban and touristy, we moved to Alma, Colorado (which holds the distinction of having the highest elevation of any town in the US), before settling in Ridgway, Colorado, in the foothills of the San Juan Mountains, in 1980. Our company, Advance Canvas Design, soon outgrew its manufacturing space in the renovated and historic Sherbino theatre in downtown Ridgway. In 1994, with the assistance of the Montrose Economic Development, we bought a 6,000 sq ft (550 sq m) building in downtown Montrose, Colorado. In only six years the company again outgrew its space and moved to a larger, 10,000 sq ft (900 sq m) facility in the summer of 2000.

Our growing manufacturing business prides itself on producing affordable alternatives to traditional housing. Affordable housing and

SPEND THE DAY KAYAKING, THEN SNUGGLE DOWN IN A YURT IN RIDGWAY STATE PARK, COLORADO, USA

entrepreneurship are two intrinsic values of the American heart and soul, and we have managed to combine these two ideals. The inspiration and design for the distinctive structures has its roots in the history and tradition of nomadic cultures. Our Earthworks Tipis are patterned after the three-pole Lakota design, with the addition of distinctive Cheyenne style smoke flaps. Advance Yurts are modern updates of the nomadic Mongolian round tents, known as *gers* or yurts.

Both tipis and yurts are gaining acceptance and popularity as comfortable and durable options for summer camps, guides, campgrounds, and weekend cabins. In many areas of the US, yurts provide backcountry getaways for both summer and winter adventures. Where there is no main power supply, photovoltaic cells can be used for electricity, and stovepipe outlets can be fitted for ventilated heating.

For us, Advance Canvas Design is not only a business, but a vehicle for social change. Our twenty-two employees are intimately involved in the company's day-to-day operations and direction, so they form a cohesive and committed team. In exchange for their hard work, we pay them a higher than average wage that enables them to pursue their personal goals.

Of course, we experience many of the frustrations and challenges that small business owners confront on a daily basis. However, the rewards of producing quality products, providing meaningful employment, and raising our son in western Colorado justify the huge task of growing a business.

WILD PAINTED HORSES PRANCE ACROSS ILLUMINATED CANVAS TIPIS NESTLING AMONG THE SAN JUAN MOUNTAINS, OURAY, COLORADO, USA

FAMILIES, FAIRS, AND FOLK

Johnny Morris: Our cottage and family business is just down the road from Wolf Glen, in the Scottish Borders. From here we take our name – the perfect combination of Scottish and Native American images. As far as I know, we are Scotland's only producers of hand-made Sioux-style tipis.

I hadn't planned it this way. I left school, studied architecture, realised it wasn't for me, and so went travelling for a while, before deciding to spend my life outdoors. I built a bender on old quarry land belonging to Traquair House, the local "Big House", and stayed there until a friend turned up with a tipi. I liked it because he could have an open fire in the centre, and live in it all year round. The fire seemed a great advantage, so I began to make my own tipi, copying the design. It took me

six months, but I got there, and once it was done I stayed there three years, throughout a fair amount of weather. The Border winds are chilly, but tipis are really toasty in winter, if you've got an inner lining.

In the early 1990s I was making my living from odd jobs and busking – playing the mandolin in Edinburgh. Eventually after a couple of years, visiting friends began to ask about my tipi. I made one for a friend, and then, realising the gap in the market, began circulating leaflets about my hand-made tipis at music and craft fairs. Business took off from there, and it now keeps me and the family going throughout the year.

My tipis are sewn by hand or on a treadle sewing machine, using rot-and-waterproof canvas. I do all the sewing

JOHNNY MORRIS

AT NIGHT WHEN YOU LOOK UPWARD, THE TIPI POLES ALMOST TOUCH
THE STARS, AND SMOKE FLAPS OPEN OUT ON TO INKY SCOTTISH SKY

myself, and my partner Moy designs the painting for the exterior, if the client chooses to have a decorated tipi. When I'm really busy a couple of local guys help me cut and prepare the poles, strip the bark, and so on.

We take our tipis to "mainstream" fairs and events; on the "alternative scene", tipis are ten a penny! This way we let ordinary folk get a chance to be in a tipi, and maybe think more about Native American culture and lifestyle. I'm drawn to that way of life myself, but it's hard to live it here and now, so I try to make the best use of what I've learned from it.

We hire out tipis as well; that's about 50 percent of our business. They're good for parties, storytelling events, healing festivals, anything! For one couple we decorated a tipi, put down a carpet, and they signed the marriage register inside!

From the initial order, it takes me about one month to complete and deliver a tipi. Generally I turn up and show the client how to put it up for the first time – there's a knack to it. If you don't get the poles right, it won't stay strong and supported. Putting up a tipi takes about an hour, including getting the fire going, and a bit longer if there's a lining and bedding to organise.

My favourite tipi was a 16-footer (5 m) one I'd built for my family. It was well-lived in and nicely "smoked-up" inside, and then I got a request from someone for exactly that! So I sold it.

As for the future, I'd like to see the word spreading further about my tipis, and my business continuing to thrive and expand.

JOHNNY MORRIS

TL: A LANARKSHIRE FESTIVAL LINEUP TR: FLYING THE FLAG FOR WOLF GLEN AT A SCOTTISH
CONSERVATION FAIR BL: TIME TO GET UP BR: FUN AT A FAMILY FESTIVAL

FAMILY HOLIDAYS FLAVOURED WITH FANTASY

Elizabeth Tom: About ten years ago someone owed us some money and couldn't pay. They offered us instead their 18 ft (5.5 m) Sioux-style tipi, complete with lodge poles, painted interior lining, fire dogs and kettle, and that bible of the tipi enthusiast, a hardback copy of *The Indian Tipi* by Reginald and Gladys Laubin. We spent several years enjoying part-time life in a tipi, with an ever-expanding family. We now have four young children who have all spent holidays and festivals in tipis, and are as at home in a lodge as in a house – and much prefer the tipi lifestyle!

We noticed that wherever we went with a tipi, people were drawn to it as if by magic: they wanted to come up close, and preferably come inside; it exerted a powerful pull that was part fantasy, part reality. So we set up Cornish Tipi Holidays about five years ago, so that other people could combine the experience of a traditional lifestyle with the beauty of rural Cornwall, southwest England.

Our 30-odd tipis are now sited in a valley which was once a quarry, but has since become a haven for the local flora and fauna. A large freshwater lake offers swimming, boating, and fishing, with the spectacular scenery and beaches of the north Cornish coast a few minutes' drive away. Interiors are fully equipped and arranged much as our own family lodge. Guests are offered tipis either in a community setting or in spacious private clearings. We offer a family-based holiday with an authentic flavour of the natural world: starry skies and outside fires, wild flowers, and children running free.

ELIZABETH TOM

AN ALTERNATIVE TO THE PACKAGE HOLIDAY: TIPI TOURISTS LIVE LIGHTLY IN CORNWALL

SPIRIT OF MUSIC CAMP

Ingrid Crawford and Romilla: Spirit of Music camps began in 1995. Each camp runs for ten days, and we run two a year. The location is idyllic, with a view of Dartmoor, Devon, England, overlooked by a stone circle, with hill forts within two miles (3 km). Close by is the magnificent Teign valley, perfect for walks or river-swimming. We have a "welcome tent" to greet people, a main marquee, a kids' tent, and communal sleeping space around the village green, with camping beyond.

The camping fields are vehicle- and dog-free, without electricity or 21st-century distractions such as mobile phones. The focus is around the fire where meals are prepared. Music starts in the evening and people take turns to play individually or accompanied, often until dawn. We have enjoyed a large range of instruments and musical styles, with occasional dancing, from Breton to belly dancing. The feeling of unity, with eyes and smiles meeting across the fire, affects everyone deeply.

During the day there is a range of musical workshops and activities for the kids. Jam sessions go on all around the field; ideas and skills are shared. Music is always floating out of somewhere. A number of live-in vehicles turn up in the car park, but everyone is encouraged to camp. People bring a wide range of structures: tipis, yurts, benders, and tents. Some of these are full-time homes, others are temporary camping shelters.

The camp is open to all. Spirit of Music is a place to step out of mainstream life, to put down your burdens, and realise your truth undistracted.

INGRID CRAWFORD

THE COLOURFUL PAINTED CANVAS AND HANDPRINTS MARK THIS OUT AS FERGUS'S TIPI, HOME TO A BAGPIPE–PLAYING FOUNDER MEMBER OF SPIRIT OF MUSIC CAMPS, DARTMOOR, ENGLAND

HOME OF THE NOMADS

Mohammed Esaqzai Aimaq: I am a member of the Aimaq, one of the large tribes of the Kuchi people in Afghanistan. We are nomadic pastoralists with no strict migration pattern; we follow the grazing for our sheep and goats. Travelling on foot and camel, we can cover distances of hundreds of miles, over mountains, and along river valleys. Just now we are in the province of Herat, northwestern Afghanistan, but later in the year we will move to Farah province, around 125 miles (200 km) from here.

Our traditional tents are called *khaimeh*, or the larger ones *qhazdhi*. They are erected at each new camp in a few hours. We often use the same sites, so the low earth walls around the tent need not be built afresh each time. The tents themselves last between five and ten years, depending on how well they were built in the first place.

The *khaimeh* is made of a number of broad lengths of cloth woven from goats' hair (the coarse outer hair, not the soft cashmere underneath) or wool. The goat-hair ones are the best quality because they are the most hardwearing. Since we spin our own yarn on a hand spinner (like a gyroscope, not a spinning wheel), it can be any mixture of wool and hair, depending upon what is available. Our tents are black in colour, because the goats are black.

We use wooden poles – three rows of 4–6 poles, the central row being the highest. The apex of some of the tents is nearly 10 ft (3 m) high. Ridge poles connect each of the uprights. Guy ropes are attached to the

RUARAIDH PETRE

TENTS OF THE ESAKZAI AIMAQ NEAR ZENDAJAN, WESTERN AFGHANISTAN, IN A SEVERE DROUGHT

outer rows of poles, and most are modern nylon rope, though we do also use hair ropes (*rasman*) and hemp ropes. Unfortunately there is very little timber left in Afghanistan now, and replacement poles have to be imported from Pakistan and Iran, unless we can barter with a farmer who has some trees.

Our tents house the sheep and goats at night as well as the people. We build walls inside the tents to make three areas – for people, livestock, and the kitchen area. Our group travels with about 2,000 sheep, 200 goats, and 50 camels. We have a total of eight tents, each housing a family of up to eight people. The *khaimeh* tents vary in size, but the biggest *qhazdhi* is about 26 ft (8 m) square, and 10 ft (3 m) high in the middle.

The spinning and weaving of goat hair is time-consuming, so many other Kuchis are starting to patch tents with alternative materials instead of the traditional goats' hair, and to use large tarpaulins for construction. Because the area has been filled with refugees and internally displaced people for so long, Kuchi people are also using large numbers of UNHCR (UN High Commission for Refugees) tents, or tents from other relief agencies. However, our tribespeople have survived – the European explorer Wilfred Thesiger said fifty years ago that there would be no Kuchis left in a few years, and we are still here. We do suffer from extremes of climate, such as severe drought, but our systems have evolved over time, and so can stand up to many pressures.

RUARAIDH PETRE

T: THE AIMAQ RETURN TO THE SAME SITES FOR SEVERAL YEARS, AND REPAIR THE MUD WALLS, INSTEAD OF BUILDING NEW ONES EACH TIME BL: MEMBERS OF THE ESAKZAI CLAN, WITH MOHAMMED, THEIR LEADER BR: SANAM GUL REPAIRS A TENT; AIMAQ WOMEN SPIN THE YARN AND WEAVE THE CLOTH FOR THE TENTS

WHERE THE GRASS IS GREENER AND HOME IS HANDMADE

Mike Hannis: Along with the other members of the Kings Hill Collective, I live in a four-acre (1.6 ha) field in Somerset, England, in one of 16 "low-impact" canvas structures, most of which are variations on traditional benders. Bender technology dovetails perfectly with sustainable land management, allowing dwellings to emerge organically from their environment. The essential technique has remained the same for thousands of years.

To make a basic bender frame, the fat ends (1–2 in, 3–5 cm) of coppiced hazel poles are pushed into the ground 6–12 in (15–30 cm). The thin ends are woven together in pairs, either to make arches in a line for a tunnel, or joining opposite poles in a circle to make a hemisphere, or any other shape. More poles are then woven in horizontally to fill the gaps, and diagonally to add strength, and tied together securely with string wherever they cross. No two bender frames are ever the same!

The frame is covered with canvas tarpaulins, roped on to pegs to hold them down against the wind. Natural canvas is generally preferable to plastic, which is very waterproof but doesn't breathe and hence traps condensation and water vapour. For year-round occupation, insulation is important. Extra layers of tarp and blankets create air pockets which help to keep the heat in. Floors are usually covered with carpets or skins, and sometimes raised on old pallets, which give excellent insulation but can provide a dream home for unwanted rodent guests!

Our benders are heated using woodburning stoves. Chimney pipes

INGRID CRAWFORD

SPRING AT KINGS HILL, ENGLAND, IS A RIOT OF GREEN, WITH CANVAS BENDERS DOTTED
AROUND THE FIELD AND CHEERY FIRES AT NIGHT

are passed through metal plates set into the tarp. Benders are very flammable, so fire awareness is crucial. Lighting is by candles, paraffin lamps, or low-voltage lights powered by solar panels or windmills. We have a borehole for clean untreated water, and use earth closets and compost toilets.

There are at least three reasons why people choose to live at places like Kings Hill. Perhaps the most important is the drive to develop more sustainable lifestyles. We share a desire, in the words of the old cliché, to be part of the solution rather than the problem.

Secondly, a bender is an organic structure that expresses the character of its builder(s). Many people find it a very rewarding experience to live close to the earth in a dwelling they can build and maintain themselves.

Thirdly, "doing it yourself" is sometimes the only option: a bender is one of the easiest and cheapest ways to get out of the cold. Our rich Western societies create homelessness in many ways, not least by treating homes as marketable commodities. People on low incomes often cannot find affordable accommodation that meets their needs. Yet resourceful people who respond to homelessness by creating their own rudimentary dwellings from scratch find themselves in a legal minefield. We, the twenty members of the Kings Hill Collective, have recently won a seven-year legal battle to establish our right to live in benders on our land. Through cases like ours, the British planning system is finally beginning to recognise that it is possible to live simply in the countryside without destroying it.

INGRID CRAWFORD

BRIAN MONGER

MIKE HANNIS

MIKE HANNIS

AT KINGS HILL, EACH BENDER IS AS UNIQUE AS ITS OWNER, AND ALL WITHSTAND THE ENGLISH WEATHER

PROTEST AND SURVIVE

Sim: During the demonstration against road-widening in Devon, England, I stayed in the communal bender at Fairmile tree protest site. It was large and open to anybody, and there was always somebody up and moving around, whatever the hour. The bender itself was unfurnished, because we never knew when we were going to get evicted. It was heated by burners made out of old gas canisters.

Our bender was home to people's bedding and piles of communal tat — most of it things that people had left behind. As I went to sleep at night, I could hear people talking round the fire — people were always turning up. Toward the end, the camp was known internationally, and TV crews arrived regularly. We needed all the help and donations we could muster.

From my bed I could hear badgers raiding the compost at night. The woodland animals grew used to us: occasionally we'd find that a squirrel had opened a jar of peanut butter and eaten it. Once we saw one running up the tree with a huge bar of chocolate, stolen from someone's stash!

There were maybe thirty people sleeping in the communal bender toward the end, sleeping huddled together in more clothes than they walked around in. We woke up with frost on the duvet.

Our "community" had a memory of something quite ancient. Natural places that are about to be destroyed have a powerful energy that is somehow passed on to the people trying to save them. The magic comes alive, and regenerates all who stay there.

INGRID CRAWFORD

T & BL: SIMPLE LIVING AT FAIRMILE PROTEST SITE, DEVON, ENGLAND   BR: THE VEGETABLE AND HERB GARDEN, WITH A POLY–COVERED BENDER TOOLSHED

A WARM, WILD PLACE

Ingrid Crawford: The track into Beneficio leads you through eucalyptus groves out into a sunny meadow filled with tipis. A stream along one side offers washing facilities and hours of amusement for children. The footpath winds its way through the valley, past homes of canvas and sticks.

Tipis sit proudly looking out over the precipice, gleaming white in the sunshine. The Big Lodge and communal gathering space is near the top; behind it lies a vegetable garden, irrigated by a hosepipe run from the water channels. The Big Lodge is open to all. Meals are prepared twice a day – a hat is passed in the eating circles for donations to buy food, including fresh vegetables and fruit from the market in town. Some nights the Big Lodge resounds with drumbeats, guitars, and singing.

Ten years ago a couple had a vision of finding some land in Spain. They lived in Wales, where it's wet and cold in the winter, and wanted a warm, wild place to winter. They found Beneficio, and began to purchase the land. When the couple arrived, they and their friends lived as a small group in tipis. Their aim was to not lose the land's bounty and pristine beauty; their strong spiritual beliefs guided them to live very gently on the land. Only natural structures were put up, including yurts, tipis, and benders. The land in between was left alone respectfully, except for narrow interconnecting pathways.

Though the founding couple have now left, some of the original dwellers still live at Beneficio. The land has now been paid for, and is home to a variety of international travellers.

INGRID CRAWFORD

VARIED DWELLINGS AT BENEFICIO, SOUTHERN SPAIN. T: A SIMPLE YURT IN ITS VERDANT GARDEN
BL: PAINTED LODGE FROM DRAGON FESTIVAL BR: BIG LODGE WHERE MEALS ARE COOKED

PERMACULTURE PARADISE

Maria Sperring: I came to France in 1990 seeking peace, to get back to nature, and to make gardens. I found Le Blé within ten days, an old farmhouse and barn with 7 acres (3 ha) of fields, woodland, and stream. Its name came from the French title of a Colette novel I was reading, *The Ripening Seed*. Uninhabited for thirteen years, surrounded by brambles and nettles, it was still in sound condition.

Having bought Le Blé with a loan, I was penniless, twenty-six years old, alone, and unable to speak French. I set about renovating with help from WWOOF (Willing Workers on Organic Farms), DIY manuals, and guesswork, and opened a guesthouse retreat. It was hard work but the joys and rewards far outweighed the sweat and fears of the early years.

Without a regular income, I kept things simple and made the best use of available resources. Having woodland and time, I could build garden structures where purchase was impossible. First came the bender polytunnels made from woven hazel rods. The success of these led to the creation of a larger structure to provide growing space and shelter for campers: an "inside/outside" place as an agreeable alternative to being driven houseward by summer showers. Seating twenty people, it makes a marvellous dining space during workshops, as well as yielding early salads and beans in May; peppers, tomatoes, and grapes in October.

The greenhouse is octagonal, with sides 9 ft (2.8 m) long, a complement to the eight-pathed "Sun Garden" adjacent to it. There are doorways to

MARIA SPERRING

THE BENDERS WERE THE FIRST GARDEN STRUCTURES MARIA CREATED,
USING WOVEN HAZEL RODS AND POLYTUNNEL PLASTIC

the north, south, east, and west, with raised beds against the remaining four sides. The basic structure is composed of large, long-lasting chestnut stakes, with eight poles fixed to a central block of oak: this design means that no columnar support is required. The stakes are charred at the base to preserve them, dug at least 20 in (50 cm) into the ground, and packed in with broken roof tiles.

The roof and sides are filled in with hazel. Recycled baler twine is woven across the spaces to add support to the plastic without increasing weight. Strips of rag lining the roof stakes protect the plastic against chafing. I covered the roof with quality four-season poly-tunnel plastic, first laid in the sun to stretch, and then cut into four overlapping triangles. Battens of pallet wood on the outside hold it down, and the joins are sealed with transparent tape.

The sloping floor was levelled to create the four raised beds, retained with woven hazel wands. Kiwis and grape vines are planted on opposite sides, growing toward each other across the roof to give shade in summer. Herbs grow at the front borders, and a rotation of beans, salads, peppers, tomatoes, and aubergines complete the planting.

The greenhouse was completed in 1996 and withstood the violent storms of 1999. Its floor is laid with rounds of wood unsuitable for burning, wedged in using sand, with a weed barrier of old carpet underneath. This beautiful, "clean", no-maintenance surface has a large thermic mass, which helps to regulate extremes of temperature.

MARIA SPERRING

TL: THE GARDEN TOOL SHED WITH PLANT STAGING IS A RECENT ADDITION
TR, B: THE ELEGANT ARCHITECTURE OF THE OCTAGONAL GREENHOUSE

BUILDING A YURT

The traditional yurt or *ger* is a portable circular structure whose wall or *khana* consists of a number of expanded split-willow lattice sections tied together with rawhide and lashed to a single wooden door frame (which faces south away from the prevailing winds). A key structural feature is the woven "tension band" that is tied around the top of the wall to prevent the roof thrusting outward. The roof structure is then built using slim wooden roof poles (each traditionally passed through the door opening and not over the wall) that connect the top of the *khana* to a central open crown known as "the eye of heaven". Once erected, the whole structure is covered with woollen felt (up to eight layers in winter) and, in wet regions, with a firmly-bound canvas cover over the felt. Many yurts are covered with white felt as this is especially sacred to the Mongols. In summer the earth floor is covered with a thin felt rug but in winter camps wooden floor bases are used. Heating and cooking are provided by a central wood- or dung-burning fire or stove. For added ventilation in summer, the bottom of the wall covering is rolled up.

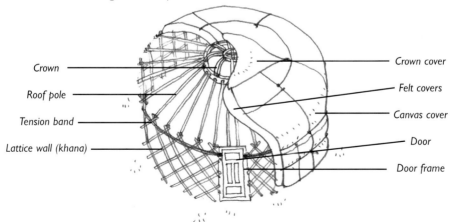

Crown

Roof pole

Tension band

Lattice wall (khana)

Crown cover

Felt covers

Canvas cover

Door

Door frame

WALLS To make the lattice wall sections (*khana*) use wooden rods, whole or split in half as slats. Traditionally these are cut in winter (coppiced) from willow trees or hazel bushes, but any sustainable straight-growing or recycled wood is good. Drill equally-spaced holes along each slat and connect all slats tightly together using string or small bolts. For ease of transport, the completed *khanas* can be folded. Once the *khana* is erected in a circle, a canvas, rope, or wire "tension band" must be tied around the top to contain the outward thrust of the roof.

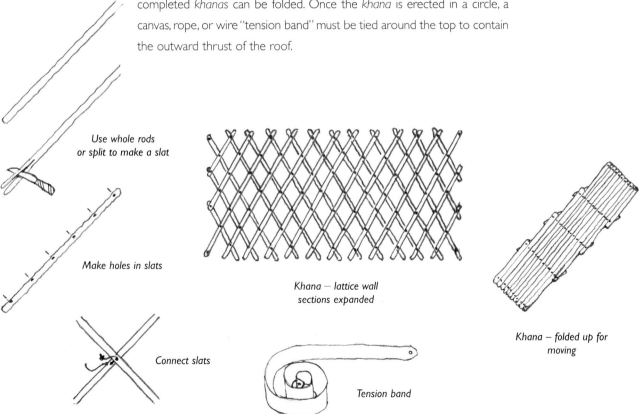

Use whole rods
or split to make a slat

Make holes in slats

Connect slats

Khana — lattice wall
sections expanded

Tension band

Khana — folded up for
moving

ROOF Using straight poles to make a Mongolian roof, taper one end to fit into the sockets around the circular "crown" (see below), and at the other end, drill two holes and tie a string loop to fit over the crossed tops of the slats of the *khana*. For a Kyrgyz roof use curved roof poles. To make these, strip the bark from green saplings, steam one end of these, and curve the steamed end in a bending jig.

CROWN The most difficult part to make! For the Mongolian crown, use separate curved pieces of wood and join them together with mortise and tenon joints. As it is heavy, support it with two uprights. Then drill and cut a series of equally spaced holes around the edge to take the roof poles. Square holes (with square roof-pole ends) are best as they prevent the roof from twisting. For an authentic Mongolian finish, paint the crown, roof poles, and uprights with polychrome designs. For the Kyrgyz crown, steam-bend two lengths of split green wood around a curved template and leave for a week. Lash or glue and dowel the ends together, cut the roof-pole holes, and brace the middle with thin pliable rods in a traditional cross-shaped design.

Mongol straight roof pole

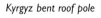

Kyrgyz bent roof pole

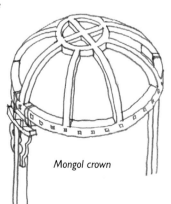

Mongol crown

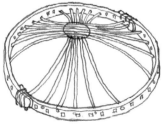

Kyrgyz crown

DOOR Make a simple Kyrgyz-style de-mountable door frame from four round-wood posts that slot together. Fix to this a door made of canvas or felt weighted at the bottom. Alternatively, have a grander, paneled-wood, Mongolian-style door. Fixed to a solid frame, this can be single or double and looks wonderful when carved and painted.

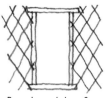

Round wood door frame

COVER Although a traditional cover is made of layers of felt, you can make a simple yurt cover using waterproof canvas. Erect the complete yurt frame and make a canvas wall to fit the *khana*. Then, laying a few lengths of overlapping canvas over the roof at a time, pin these in position, take down and sew together, and repeat until they cover the roof. Finally trim, fold, and sew the crown opening and ends, allowing a good overlap with the wall cover. Make a star–shaped crown cover of canvas with clear plastic windows and metal flue collar.

Wood panel door

Felt door

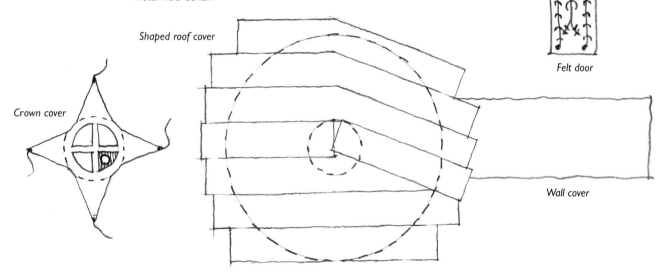

Shaped roof cover

Crown cover

Wall cover

PUTTING UP A KYRGYZ YURT

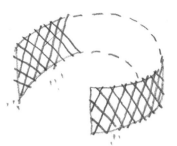

1 Erect the khana

1 Tie *khana* wall sections together and erect in a circle.
2 Lash door frame to the *khana* and tie the tension band around the top.
3 Insert three roof poles into the crown, lift up, and loop ends over the *khana*.

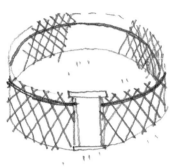

2 Add the door frame and tension band

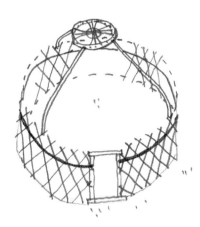

3 Raise the crown

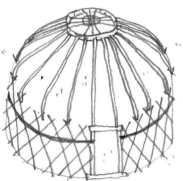

4 Slot in the roof poles

4 Add the remaining roof poles to complete the frame.
5 Add the wall and roof covers. Make tight and secure with ropes and pegs. Tie crown cover in position. Fix felt door.

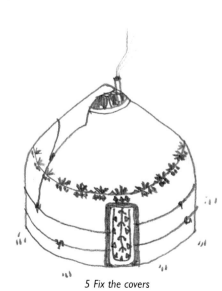

5 Fix the covers

TRADITIONAL INTERIOR Traditionally, everyone and everything has their appointed place inside a yurt. Men, together with their saddles, guns, and ropes, are on the west side near the hearth; the "place of honour" for important guests is between the hearth and altar. Women and the cooking utensils, churn, cradle, and clothes occupy the east side. The young and new-born animals are often put near the door. The north, the most sacred place, is reserved for the altar.

MODERN INTERIOR Inside a modern Mongolian *ger*, the open fire has been replaced by a metal stove. Rugs and furs on the floor have been replaced by beds. Cupboards and chests of drawers replace boxes and storage bags. And, in winter, a wooden floor is used. Electric light and TV, sometimes solar- or battery-powered, are popular. The altar, however, is still there, with religious icons, and photos of beloved horses, family, and friends!

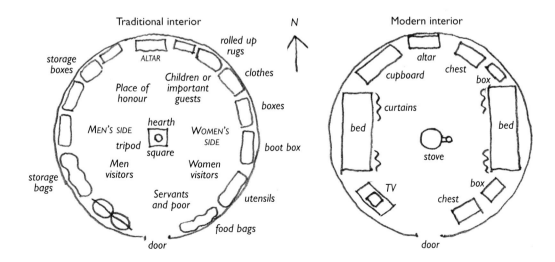

BUILDING A TIPI

The tipi is the most ingenious conical tent ever devised. Traditionally it was owned, fabricated, and erected by female members of the tribe. The plan of a tipi is not a true circle: it is actually egg-shaped, with the wider part toward the rear. The cone also tilts backward, with its steeper rear side braced against the prevailing westerly winds. The fire is not central but positioned a little forward to be under the smoke hole. Traditional hide covers were tanned and scraped thin to reduce weight and let in more light; eight to ten hides being needed for a small 12 ft (3.6 m) diameter tipi. By the late 1800s lighter canvas covers began to replace hide. When the cover was complete it was hoisted on to the frame and secured in position: the door always facing east toward the morning sun and away from prevailing winds. Moveable "smoke flaps" at the top greatly assisted smoke ventilation.

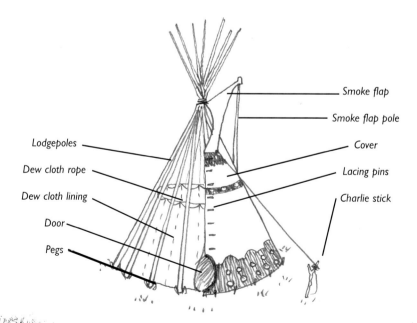

Smoke flap

Smoke flap pole

Lodgepoles

Cover

Dew cloth rope

Dew cloth lining

Lacing pins

Charlie stick

Door

Pegs

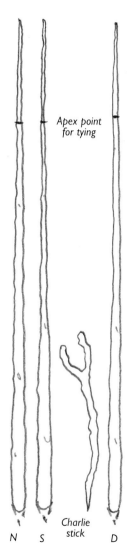

Apex point
for tying

Charlie
stick

N   S   D

Tripod poles (north, south, and door poles) and charlie stick (see page 88)

POLES The frame of the tipi is made of straight wooden poles referred to as "lodgepoles" – the preferred wood being from the lodgepole pine. But any straight-growing tree, such as eucalyptus, can also be used. The best poles are cut from woods or forest at the end of winter and beginning of spring. Be careful to cause as little damage to the woodland ecosystem as possible. Green poles are easier to work and last longer than seasoned poles. They must be as straight and slender as possible. Cut off all the branches flush with the trunk and, working from the butt to the top, use a draw knife to debark the poles (much easier if the wood is "green"). After seasoning for three weeks, sand the poles smooth. This helps raindrops to run straight down them and not drip on the cover. Shape the pole bases into points so they can pierce the ground, and tie streamers to the tops to dance in the wind.

For an 18 ft (5.5 m) diameter tipi you will need 15 poles (including the lifting pole) each about 25 ft (7.5 m) long. You will also need two smoke flap poles, which are a little shorter and do not need to be as straight.

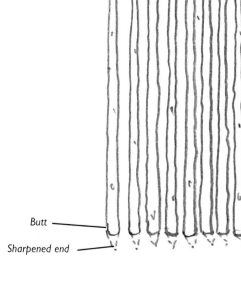

Top

Streamers

Butt

Sharpened end

COVER Use medium-weight white cotton canvas so the interior will be well lit in daylight. To make the cover, lay strips of canvas on the ground, sew the edges together (preferably with an industrial sewing machine), and then cut off and hem the ends to make the semicircular shape.

Measuring from the middle of the longest strip, cut out and sew two smoke flaps and two halves of the door opening. Punch the lacing pin holes and sew around their edges.

Add two canvas pockets and tie tapes to the smoke flaps to take the smoke flap poles, and sew a reinforced "lifting triangle" plus tapes for the lifting pole. Complete the cover by adding peg loops around the bottom.

If you want to paint a design on the cover, do this with it spread out on the ground.

Make the "dew cloth" from tapered pieces of canvas, sewn together with ties top and bottom. Tie the top and bottom to "lining ropes" lashed to the inside of each pole.

The canvas door, stiffened with rods at top and base, is fixed to the cover with lacing pins and to the ground with two pegs. In rainy weather, cover the pole tops with a "rain hat" made from a canvas square.

MAKING THE COVER

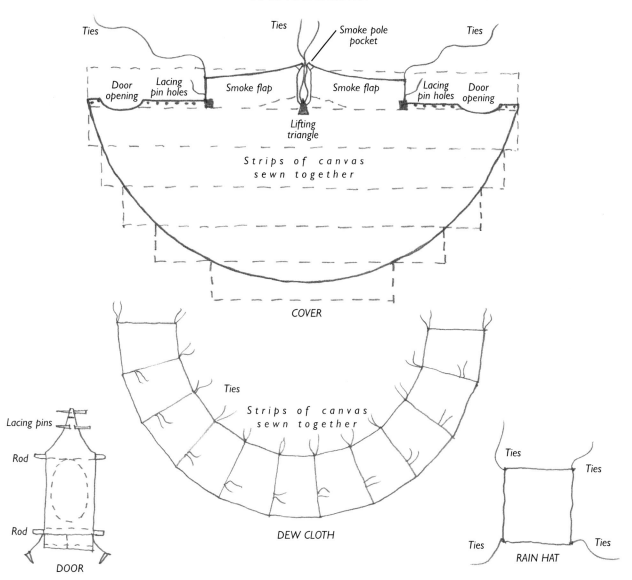

Ties

Ties

Ties

Smoke pole pocket

Door opening — Lacing pin holes — Smoke flap — Smoke flap — Lacing pin holes — Door opening

Lifting triangle

S t r i p s   o f   c a n v a s   s e w n   t o g e t h e r

COVER

Lacing pins

Rod

Rod

DOOR

Ties

S t r i p s   o f   c a n v a s   s e w n   t o g e t h e r

DEW CLOTH

Ties

Ties

Ties

Ties

RAIN HAT

PUTTING UP A TIPI

1 Make the tripod

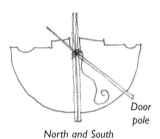

North and South poles

Door pole

Spread cover face down, lie N, S poles together, place D pole over them. Tie poles where they cross the triangle in the cover. Leave plenty of free rope.

2 Erect the tripod

S   *N*

Door

Now lift the tripod and position the splayed poles, pushing them into the ground. (Door traditionally faces east.)

3 Add the poles

Add and peg the other poles, except the lifting pole. Wind the free rope around the apex and anchor to the ground.

4 Lift the cover

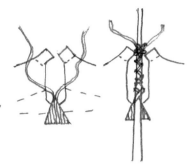

Lie the lifting pole down the middle of the cover and tie it to the lifting triangle.

5 Fix the cover

Fold the cover around the lifting pole and heave it into place, unfurl it around the poles, and close the front with lacing pins.

6 Fix the dewcloth

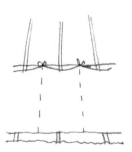

Tie the dew cloth to the top and bottom rope attached to each pole, and attach the door.

7 Raise the smoke flaps

Lift up the smoke flaps with two poles and adjust their position by tying the two tapes to a forked "charlie stick".

8 Use the rain hat

In rainy weather use the rain hat to cover the top of the poles.

TRADITIONAL INTERIOR Within the egg-shaped plan of the tipi there were generally areas for men on the north side and women on the south side and specific places for male and female guests. The altar, a small "square of mellowed earth" behind the hearth, represented Mother Earth, and sweet incense burned there carried prayers to the Ones Above.

TRADITIONAL COVERS   Some tipi covers were painted with designs, following a ritual dream. The lower part, usually painted red, represented the earth; the middle area the sky, and a dark band at the top the night sky and the stars.

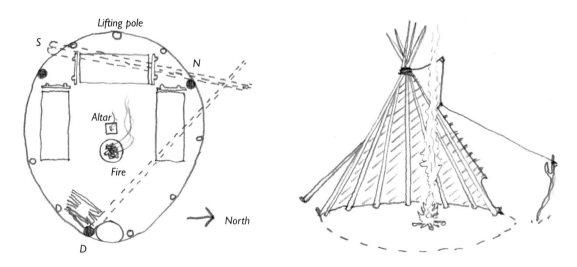

Interior showing the forward fire
position under the smoke hole.

BUILDING A BENDER

Bent-pole houses or benders are the simplest and most universal form of shelter used all over the world from Africa to Europe and the Americas. Made from cut sapling uprights bent over and tied together at the top, these structures may be circular, oblong, or tunnel shaped. Coverings are many and various including grass, rush, or reed mats, bark, scrub, and yucca leaves depending on local culture, climate, and materials. Sometimes the frame was left standing from year to year at seasonal camp sites and only the coverings rolled or packed up and removed. In the Americas, the "sweat-house" or "purification lodge" was constructed in this way and covered with either buffalo hide or cloth. Rocks heated in a fire outside were then carried via a "sacred path" through the east-facing entrance and placed in a central pit. Water ladled over them produced a hot steamy atmosphere that, together with prayers and songs, purified body and soul.

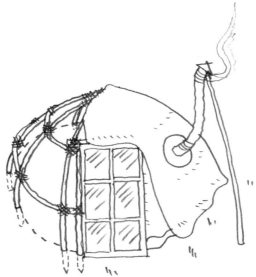

Measure and clear a circular or oblong-shaped area on the ground. Dig a drainage trench around the edge with a downhill gully. Mark rod positions. From the woods cut long, straight slender "green" saplings (coppiced hazel is good) and sharpen the thicker butt ends. Hammer a wooden or metal spike into the ground to make deep rod holes. Push the butt end of the sapling rods into each hole, making each pole lean slightly outward. Taking opposite poles, bend them over so the ends overlap well and tie them together firmly to form arches. Do the same for all the other poles to complete the domed structure. To each upright around the structure, tie two or three horizontal "stringers" made of smaller pliable saplings, leaving a space for the door. Weave them in and out of the uprights for extra strength. A door and window (preferably recycled) can be added at this stage. Traditional coverings, as above, may be used but pieces of canvas are now more common. Drape the canvas over the structure and around the door and window and secure to pegs in the ground. If no door or window is added, just roll up the canvas to make a simple doorway. Use a stove for heating and cooking but be sure to make a metal collar for the stovepipe.

Wigwam

Sweat lodge

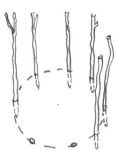

Sapling rod circle

Bent sapling arches

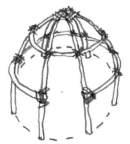

Horizontal "stringers"

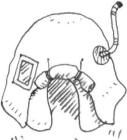

Canvas cover

RESOURCES

Note on telephone numbers
For national calls, *do not* dial the country code inside the first pair of brackets. Dial the prefix inside the second pair, followed by the rest of the number.

For international calls to Europe, dial the country code inside the first pair of brackets, but *not* the European prefix (0) inside the second pair. Follow this up with the rest of the number.

For international calls to the US, dial the whole number including all prefixes. Note that numbers beginning with 800 are free inside the US only.

YURTS

Paul King
Woodland Yurts
80 Coleridge Vale Road South
Clevedon
North Somerset
BS21 6PG
England, UK
Tel: (00 44) (0) 1275 879705
Website:
www.woodlandyurts.com
email:
yurts@woodlandyurts.freeserve.
  co.uk
Handcrafted yurts made to order

William Coperthwaite
The Yurt Foundation
Machaisport,
Maine 04655
USA
Sells reasonably priced plans for building your own yurt, and calendars. Write for information about workshops or help with your yurt.

Dan Neumeyer
Jade Design/Build
PO Box 757
Langley
Washington 98260
USA
Tel: (001) (360) 321 5990
Fax: (001) (360) 221 7993
Website:
www.JadeDesignBuild.com
email: dan@jadedesignbuild.com
Jade Design/Build designs and builds wooden yurts based on Bill Coperthwaite's designs

Hal Wynne-Jones
Hullasey Barn
Tarlton
Cirencester
Gloucestershire
England, UK
Tel/Fax: (00 44) (0)1285 770773
Yurts for sale. May be hired out for functions, parties, etc – fully furnished, lit, and heated. Service includes delivery, erection, and dismantling

Peter Whiteman
Lower Turley Farm
Cullompton
Devon
EX15 1NA
England, UK
Tel: (00 44) (0)1884 32234
Yurts made to order

The Australian National Yurt
  Project
The Australian Forum for Textile
  Arts
PO Box 38 The Gap
Queensland 4061
Australia
Tel: (00 61) (0) 7 3300 6491
Fax: (00 61) (0) 7 3300 2148
Website:
www.ggcreations.com.au/tafta/
email: tafta@uq.net.au
or the coordinator of the Australian Yurt Project, Martien Van Zuilen at martienvz@hotmail.com
Further information about the Australian yurt and bookings. Postcards with images of the Yurt for sale; all money raised goes back into the project

Coastal Yurts
Oregon State Parks Info Center
Tel: (001) 800 551 6949
Brochures, maps, and park descriptions

Reservation Center:
PO Box 500
Portland
OR 97207-0500
USA
Tel: (001) 800 452 5687
Telephone Device for the Deaf:
(001) 800 858 9659
Website: www.prd.state.or.us
Reservations accepted year-round up to 9 months ahead

Pacific Yurts Inc.
77456 Hwy 99 South
Cottage Grove
Oregon 97424
USA
Phone: (001) 800 9440240
Fax: (001) (541) 942 0508
Website: www.yurts.com
email: yurt@pacinfo.com
Modern US-style yurts for sale; also supplied to Oregon State Parks for rent to campers

Peaceful Valley
Alternative holidays in Turkey
12 Trinity Road
Aberystwyth
Ceredigion SY23 1LU
Wales, UK
Tel/Fax: (00 44) (0) 1970 626821
Website: www.huzurvadisi.com
email:
huzurvadisi@compuserve.com

Huzur Vadisi
Gokceovacik
Gocek 48310
Fethiye
Turkey
Tel: (00 90) (0) 252 645 2419
Relaxing yurt-based holidays
with/without courses in yoga, Tai
Chi, dance, etc

Stephanie Bunn
Windsor Cottage
Felixstowe Ferry
Suffolk
IP11 9RZ
England, UK
Information on feltmaking and the
Kyrgyz yurt

Advance Canvas Design
28 W. South Street
PO Box 1626
Montrose
Colorado 81402
USA
Tel: (001) 800 288 3190
Tel: (001) (970) 240 2111
Fax: (001) (970) 240 2146
Website:
www. AdvanceCanvas.com
email: info@advancecanvas.com
Makers of Earthworks Tipis and
Advance Yurts; also suppliers of
yurts to Ridgway State Park,
Mancos State Park, Golden Gate
State Park, Pearl Lake State Park,
La Foret State Forest, all in
Colorado

Colorado State Parks
1313 Sherman Street, Rm 618
Denver
Colorado 80203

USA
Tel: (001) (303) 866 3437
Website: http://parks.state.co.us/
– click on yurts and cabins link

Ridgway State Park
28555 Highway 550
Ridgway
Colorado 81432
Tel: (001) (970) 626 5822
Website:
http://parks.state.co.us/ridgway/
    yurts.htm
email: ridgway.park@state.co.us

TIPIS

Johnny Morris
Wolf Glen Tipis
Williamhope Cottage
Clovenfords
Galashiels
TD1 3LL
Scotland, UK
Tel: (00 44) (0) 1896 850390
Website:
www.btinternet.com/~wolf.glen
email: wolfglentipis@amserve.net
Handmade tipis for sale and hire
for parties, festivals, etc. Delivery,
erection, and dismantling included
in service

Elizabeth Tom
Cornish Tipi holidays
Tregeare
Pendoggett
St Kew
Cornwall
PL30 3LW
England, UK
Tel: (00 44) (0) 1208 880781
Fax: (00 44) (0) 1208 880487

Website:
www.cornish-tipi-holidays.co.uk
email:
info@cornish-tipi-holidays.co.uk
Family-based holidays in tipis in
rural Cornwall

Spirit of Music Camps
Romilla
England, UK
Tel: (00 44) (0) 1884 855497

TENTS AND BENDERS

Kings Hill Bender Development
East Pennard
Shepton Mallet
Somerset
BA4 6TR
England, UK
email: mhannis@ukonline.co.uk
No new members are needed at
Kings Hill at present

Fairmile Protest Site
This protest site no longer exists.
For details of UK protest action,
contact SchNEWS
c/o on the fiddle
PO Box 2600, Brighton
East Sussex
BN2 2DX
England, UK
Tel/fax: (00 44) (0) 1273 685913
Website: www.schnews.org.uk/
email: schnews@brighton.co.uk

Beneficio
The exact location is not
publicised. Go to southern Spain
and ask a fellow-traveller for
directions.

Maria Sperring
Le Blé en Hèrbe
Puissetier
23350 La Celette
France
Tel/Fax: (00 33) (0) 5 55 80 62 83
email:
maria.sperring@gofornet.com
Farm guesthouse retreat/camping/
self-catering/workshop
programme/organic garden work
exchange scheme

GENERAL

International Feltmakers'
    Association
Chair: Sheila Smith
17 Cleveland Way
Carlton Miniott
Thirsk
North Yorkshire
YO7 4LN
England, UK
Tel/Fax: (00 44) (0)1845 523340
Website: www.feltmakers.org.uk/
email: sheils@miniott.demon.co.uk
Membership and subscriptions to
Echoes, the Association's journal

Association for Environment
    Conscious Building
www.aecb.net/index.htm

Ecological Design Association
Website: www.edaweb.org
email: ecological@designassocia
    tion.freeserve.co.uk
(Founded by David Pearson.
Publishes EcoDesign magazine.)

INDEX

Bold page numbers indicate photographs

FURTHER READING

How to Build a Yurt Factsheet Centre for Alternative Technology Publications, Machynlleth, Wales, 1997

How to Build your Low Impact Dwelling Structure Constructor, Yorkshire, 1997

How to Make a Tipi Tipsheet 10, Centre for Alternative Technology Publications, Machynlleth, Wales [no date]

BLUE EVENING STAR **Making Tipis & Yurts** Lark Books, Asheville, NC, 2000

CHARNEY, LEONARD **Build a Yurt** Sterling Publishing Co. Inc, New York, 1974

FAEGRE, TORVALD **Tents: Architecture of the Nomads** John Murray, London [no date]

FREEDMAN, RUSSELL **Buffalo Hunt**, Holiday House, New York, 1995 (reissue)

HUNT, W BEN **The Complete How-to Book of Indiancraft** Hungry Minds IDG, New York, 1973

KING, P R **Build Your Own Yurt** P R King publishing, Clevedon, Somerset, 1997

KING, P R **The Weekend Yurt** P R King publishing, Clevedon, Somerset, 1999

KING, PAUL **The Complete Yurt Handbook** Eco-Logic Books, Bristol 2001

LAUBIN, REGINALD & GLADYS **The Indian Tipi** University of Oklahoma Press, Norman, OK, 1977

NABOKOV, PETER & EASTON, ROBERT **Native American Architecture** Oxford University Press Inc., New York & Oxford, 1989

PEDERSEN, GORM **Afghan Nomads in Transition** Thames and Hudson, London, 1994

SHEMIE, BONNIE **Houses of Hide and Earth** Tundra Books, Plattsburg, New York, 1991

STEWART, STANLEY **In the Kingdom of Genghis Khan** HarperCollins, London, 2000

WHITEFIELD, PATRICK **Tipi Living** Permanent Publications, Hampshire 2000 (distributed in the US by Chelsea Green)

WHITEMAN, PETER "More experience in making felt for yurts" in **Echoes** (journal of the International Feltmakers' Association, UK branch) Vol 48, 1997

ACKNOWLEDGMENTS

Gaia Books is deeply indebted to each and every contributor to and photographer of the stories featured in this book. Gaia Books would also like to thank the many people who have helped with yurt, tipi, and bender research, mainly behind the scenes and for no personal gain:
Mary De Danan, EcoDesign magazine, Roger Frood, Dennis Gould, the Green Shop, John Harris, Diana Humphrey, Chip Meneley, Gerardine Munroe, Ian O'Reilly, Sylvia Pearson, Charlie Ryrie for her early work , Debbie Sayers, Helen Street, Stroud Bookshop, Marion Webster

David Pearson would like to thank the Gaia team: especially *Helena Petre* for her tireless work in researching and compiling the fascinating stories of the contributors; *Bridget Morley* for her talented and imaginative design; *Katherine Pate* for her professional editorial work; *Lyn Kirby* for production control; *Patrick Nugent* for project management, and *Lynn Bresler* for proofreading and the index.
I would also like to thank everyone at Chelsea Green Publishing for their helpful and enthusiastic support.